Virtual Remote Audits

From Planning to Implementation

2nd revised edition

AF235768

Virtual Remote Audits

From Planning to Implementation

Dr. Roland Scherb, MBA, PhD

2nd revised edition

IMPRINT

Bibliografische Information der Deutschen Nationalbibliothek:
Die Deutsche Nationalbibliothek verzeichnet diese Publikation in der Deutschen Nationalbibliografie; detaillierte bibliografische Daten sind im Internet über http://dnb.dnb.de abrufbar.

© 2021 Dr. Roland Scherb, MBA, PhD

Übersetzung: Dr. Cornelia Maier, PhD
Korrektorat: Petra Scherb
Grafik und Satz: Fritz-Michael Pückler

Herstellung und Verlag: BoD – Books on Demand, Norderstedt

ISBN: 978-3-7543-0166-1

FREE DOWNLOAD

See the **free download website** for this book for supplemental information: Download a **checklist** and **audit template** at the following link:

www.PeRoBa.de/RemoteAuditEnglish

CONTENT

FOREWORD

The author of this book is the Managing Director of PeRoBa Unternehmensberatung (Management Consultancy) GmbH (LLC), who has been performing audits as an auditor and consultant since the 90s. In 2005, he conducted the first "remote audit" in the form of a phone conference through a telephone conference station.

As a lecturer and coach, the author presents remote audits as another tool for performing audits. Based on plenty of discussions and conversations with auditors and users, the definition of remote audits is very important in this context.

Many solutions currently offered on the market hail from the "service" area and are now also being advertised for remote audits due to increasing demand. However, everybody needs to think their utilization over precisely as further requirements will be relevant for quality management.

The idea to write this book was conceived of at the beginning of 2014. However, the decisive moment occurred in 2017 due to an overseas auditing assignment. The return trip took approximately 40 hours because of extremely bad weather conditions that caused delays and flight cancelations. From these circumstances, the idea to make remote audits possible through an efficient tool resulted, and it was realized by an invention the author developed by himself.

In 2020, there was an unintended and inadvertent development boost due to COVID-19 since lots of companies further advanced digitalization and working from home. This edition is supposed to point out and elaborate on the significance of remote audits.

1 REMOTE AUDITS

Starting from the first lockdown in March 2020, quite a few things regarding company processes have changed due to the COVID-19 pandemic.

That impacted the area of management systems as well. Audits could not be performed any more as originally planned.

On a supplementary basis, safety and security restrictions were altered within companies, and regular audits on-site have usually become impossible or only feasible under severe limitations due to traveling restrictions.

Audits are well described in DIN EN ISO 9000:2015-11; citing subsequently from standard section 2.4.2 on developing the quality management system (QMS), 5th paragraph, page 24,

"Auditing is a means of evaluating the effectiveness of the QMS, in order to identify risks and to determine the fulfilment of requirements. In order for audits to be effective, tangible and intangible evidence needs to be collected. Actions are taken for correction and improvement based upon analysis of the evidence gathered. The knowledge gained could lead to innovation, taking QMS performance to higher levels."[1]

Remote auditing is a special kind of auditing, which needs to meet all the other requirements on auditing as a matter of principle in order to generate efficient results in terms of quality management.

The performance of remote audits can also constitute a reasonable solution so that audits can still be conducted in spite of the existing restrictions.

---

[1] DIN e.V., 2015

1.1. THE DEFINITION OF REMOTE AUDITS & REGULATIONS

DIN EN ISO 19011[2] mentioned remote audits as such for the first time in the English version in 2011. They were further elaborated on in the version of 2018 and referred to as *"virtuelle Audits"* (virtual audits) or *"Fernaudits"* (remote audits) in the German translation. In Annex A.16 of ISO 19011, virtual or remote audits are described more precisely. It is stated there, that remote audits may be performed irrespectively of *"Remote audit activities are performed at any place other than the location of the auditee, regardless of the distance."[3]*

In standard section 5.5.3 of ISO 19011:2018, remote audits are depicted in more detail, *"Audits can be performed on-site, remotely or as a combination. The use of these methods should be suitably balanced, based on, among others, consideration of associated risks and opportunities."[4]*

Meanwhile, other regulations have been providing information on remote audits, too.

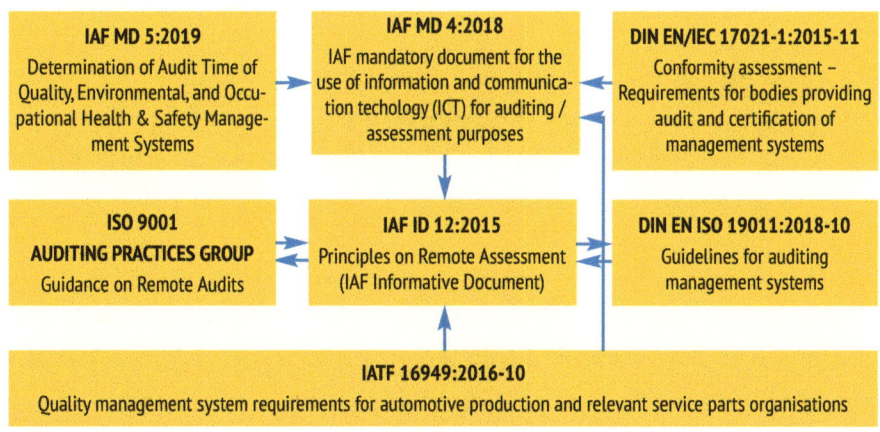

Figure 1: Requirements from regulations – as of December 2020

---

[2] DIN EN ISO 19011:2018-10 – Guidelines for auditing management systems (ISO 19011:2018)

[3] DIN e.V., 2018

[4] ISO 19011, 2018, P. 34, Section 5.5.3 second paragraph (DIN e.V., 2018)

IAF MD4:2018[5]

IAF MANDATORY DOCUMENT FOR THE USE OF INFORMATION AND COMMUNICATION TECHNOLOGY (ICT) FOR AUDITING/ASSESSMENT PURPOSES.

Requirements on remote audits are formulated in "4.1 Security and Confidentiality" and in "4.2 Process requirements". It is mentioned here under point 4.2.5 that impacts on the auditing time may result from determining the auditing and assessment time for additional requirements.

Furthermore, in this document, reference is made to the following computer assisted auditing techniques (CAAT) as remote auditing techniques, for instance:
- Telephone conferences
- Sessions on the internet
- Interactive web-based communication
- Electronic remote access to the documentation of the management systems and / or the management system processes.

IAF MD 5:2019[6]

IAF Mandatory Document – DETERMINATION OF AUDIT TIME OF QUALITY, ENVIRONMENTAL, AND OCCUPATIONAL HEALTH & SAFETY MANAGEMENT SYSTEMS.

In the preceding version, remote auditing activities had still been limited to 30 %. However, this restriction is no longer existing in the present version. Remote auditing techniques may be used without any time limitations now.

---

[5] https://european-accreditation.org/wp-content/uploads/2018/10/232846.IAF-MD4-2008-CAAT_Pub.pdf

[6] https://european-accreditation.org/wp-content/uploads/2018/10/IAFMD5QMSEMSAuditDurationIssue311062015.pdf

DIN EN ISO/IEC 17021-1:2015-11[7]

Conformity assessment – Requirements for bodies providing audit and certification of management systems – Part 1: Requirements (ISO/IEC 17021-1:2015); German and English version EN ISO/IEC 17021-1:2015.

9.2.3.2 d) states that remote audits need to be identified in the audit plan, and the author considers this a requirement that ought to be both crucial and fundamental.

ISO/IEC 17021-3:2017(EN)[8]

ISO/IEC 17021-3:2017 specifies additional competence requirements for personnel involved in the audit and certification process for quality management systems (QMS) and complements the existing requirements of ISO/IEC 17021-1.

IAF ID 12:2015[9]

IAF Informative Document – Principles on Remote Assessment. In this document, remote assessments are defined (see 3.1), and under point 5.3 et seq., possible application and utilization scenarios are presented.

ISO 9001 Auditing Practices Group[10]

Guidance on: REMOTE AUDITS, an introduction to remote audits, which includes a checklist of exemplary risks with regard to the performance of remote audits.

Finally, there are additional provisions to be mentioned in order to carry out audits under medical requirements:

---

[7] https://www.beuth.de/en/standard/din-en-iso-iec-17021-1/231355332

[8] https://www.iso.org/obp/ui/#iso:std:iso-iec:17021:-3:ed-1:v1:en

[9] https://www.iaf.nu/upFiles/IAFID12PrinciplesRemoteAssessment22122015.pdf

[10]https://committee.iso.org/files/live/sites/tc176/files/documents/ISO%209001%20Auditing%2 0Practices%20Group%20docs/Auditing%20General/APG-Remote_Audits.pdf

MDCG 2020-4[11]

Guidance on temporary extraordinary measures related to medical device notified body audits during COVID-19 quarantine orders and travel restrictions.

Directions for the activities of expert agencies in the AZAV area, as regards dealing with the risks of spreading COVID-19[12]

This directive points out that remote audits are not permitted with respect to first and renewed provider licenses in the AZAV area.

1.2. DIFFERENT KINDS OF REMOTE AUDITS

At present, there are various definitions of remote audits. An internet research on the search term "definition of remote audit" resulted in 9 hits in German.

However, none of them was actually helpful for defining remote audits. Based on DIN EN ISO 9000 and DIN EN ISO 19011 as well as our experience with the remote audits we had already conducted, we came up with the following definitions:

Fully Remote Audit

The audit is conducted as a fully remote audit. Everything is done electronically, including the audit planning, the actual performance, the completion, and the delivery of the audit report.

During the entire audit, the auditor and the audited party are working from different locations.

---

[11]https://ec.europa.eu/health/sites/health/files/md_sector/docs/md_mdcg_2020_4_nb_audits_covid-19_en.pdf

[12] https://www.dakks.de/en/pressrelease/dakks-adopts-safety-measures-suspension-of-on-site-assessments.html

Partly Remote Audit

Just those parts of the audit which are suitable for remote performance are conducted remotely, not the entire audit.

With this variation, only parts of the audit take place on-site, or the auditor and co-auditor respectively the experts do the auditing working from different locations. The following options are possible, for instance:

- The co-auditor is on-site and audits relevant persons, activities, or processes.
- Executives or employees of the organization are interviewed, and the documents which are relevant for this purpose are analyzed.
- An auditor, who is not on-site, audits relevant persons, activities or processes with the help of a co-auditor, who is at the location of the organization and provides assistance via digital technologies.

Remote Follow-up Audits

They are follow-up audits for proving that measures have been implemented, etc. As a rule, they come after an audit that has already been conducted and take place as remote audits over critical deviations so that e.g., the auditors needn't travel to the site again.

Expert Remote Audits

They will be an option if and when an expert who needn't be physically present during the entire auditing time is required.

Telecommunication technologies make it possible for the external expert to take part in the audit, and they reduce financial expenses or can provide viable options and help in cases when the audit could otherwise not be conducted for certain other reasons.

Thus, the presence of a technological expert might just be necessary for a period of 2 hours in order to analyze a certain audit aspect, for example.

1.3. OPPORTUNITIES AND RISKS OF REMOTE AUDITS

The upward revaluation of the audit plan constitutes an **opportunity**. The remote audit has to be included in the audit plan, and alternatives ranging up to a fallback plan need to be provided in case of any problems or malfunctions.

Furthermore, utilization of the said new technologies makes for crucial advantages in terms of time and costs. Irrespectively of the distance and the resulting traveling time, an audit can factually be conducted at any time.

The reduction of impacts affecting the environment, meaning the improvement of the ecological assessment and of the carbon footprint, is also tantamount to positive scale effects accompanying remote audits.

The remote audit is also a significant opportunity for any auditor who is supposed to perform an audit in a crisis area, be it affected by war, terrorism, or pandemics.

The possibility to conduct remote audits flexibly may also be tantamount to an opportunity. For instance, remote audits can provide the option to have audits that were not planned or announced in advance if authorities have imposed new regulations and if conformity is at issue. With the aid of remote audits, it is possible to perform live checks in real time in order to see whether someone has reliably implemented the respective applicable standards.

That is very different from a traditional on-site audit when the date is scheduled beforehand, and because of the traveling time as well as the notice and time to prepare, the audited party might be able to take certain precautions in order to insure a successful pass during the audit.

However, during remote audits, there is a significant **risk** with regard to technological framework conditions (ICT). As the audit is conducted virtually, meaning via computer, there will be increased requirements on the technological framework conditions when it comes to telecommunication, such as sufficient bandwidth.

Among other things, computers or mobile devices with phone and video capabilities as well as stable WLAN coverage for mobile use are needed.

The utilization of a remote audit should be evaluated carefully, especially if technological problems might occur. The latter must be noted and taken into account within the audit plan at any rate. Limited or partially missing human interaction amounts to a disadvantage for the auditor, too.

Even if the auditor and the audited party can see each other during a video conference, the so-called first impression won't be that accurate in virtual surroundings, other than during a personal meeting. Human interaction can solely be noticed in a limited manner, as it is not transmitted to a great extend virtually. The auditor will, therefore, just be alerted to a lesser degree by their intuition, if the body language of the auditee seems weird, and needs to be aware of that. Basically, only the face or part of the body is shown virtually, not the entire impression, other than during face-to-face meetings.

As a rule, a fully remote audit can't be recommended for performing an initial audit. If a site, a plant, or a branch office is supposed to be audited for the very first time within the framework of an internal audit, a classic on-site audit or a partly remote audit including parts during which the auditor is actually present on-site will be advisable in any case.

The question of whether a remote audit can be conducted at all must also be carefully evaluated. In this context, data privacy, safety, and confidentiality need to be made sure of. Especially in Germany respectively Europe, the General Data Protection Regulation (GDPR) must be abided by.[13]

---

[13] https://gdpr-info.eu/

REMOTE AUDIT	OPPORTUNITIES	RISKS
General	• Conservation of resources • Short-term assessment of a situation • Risk reduction in unsafe destination areas • External experts can be called in more easily and efficiently	• Missing or reduced personal contact to partner(s) • Possibly restricted vision on the part of the auditor • Interruptions through insufficient bandwidth or other IT problems • Data privacy and safety issues

Figure 2: Overview of possible opportunities and risks – in general

REMOTE AUDIT ATTENDEES	OPPORTUNITIES	RISKS
Auditor	• More efficient implementation • No additional effort over the presence of the auditors	• Lack of skills • Insufficient experience • No knowledge of the audited person
Auditee(s)	• Reduction of nervousness • Fewer disruption of processes	• Doesn't / don't take the audit seriously enough • Insufficient preparation, colleagues can help ... • Misunderstandings resulting from virtual communication

Figure 3: Overview of possible opportunities and risks – participants

TECHNOLOGIES	APPLICATION	OPPORTUNITIES	RISKS
Use of currently common tools, like, Teams, Webex, Skype, Zoom, Jitsi Meet, GoTo Meeting ...	• Conducting interviews • Virtual group meetings	• Easier connection of several locations or employees who are working from home, etc. • Reduction of travel time and costs • Geographical distances are easily overcome	• Security and confidentiality violations (screenshots, etc.) • Authentication of the participants (especially without a camera) • No autonomous visits to the relevant areas possible • Communication problems
	• Document review • Involvement of several participants	• Document review if a trip on-site is not possible or if there are significant risks in the target area • No impact of travel restrictions, no environmental issues ...	• Security and confidentiality violations (screenshots, etc.) • Potential issues with responding to related documentation requests • Possible manipulation
Tools Use of applications and tools	• Editing checklists • Providing surveys	• Possible support / simplification during the preparation phase • Preparation of the participants for the remote audit	• Authentication of the participants (especially without a camera) • Increased efforts during preparation • Possible manipulation • Efforts to train the recipient(s)
Document review offline	Review of: • Process overviews • Documented Procedures • Work instructions • Action lists ...	• Better preparation possible • Basis for audit preparation • Reduction of the audit time during the implementation	• Security and confidentiality breaches (screenshots, etc.) • Problems with the display or the presentation of formats • No direct communication • Possible manipulation
Use of camera Using video	• Review of the audit location • Assessment of processes and places	• Places that are hard to reach can be accessed more easily by the auditor • Evidence through recording can be facilitated • Good addition to follow-up audits	• The auditor is not using the camera and cannot freely decide on what is being shown • Field of view limited • Transmission of noises and volume can be impaired • No further sensory impressions possible, such as smell • Bad image quality due to insufficient bandwidth

Figure 4: Sample overview of possible opportunities and risks – ICT

2 THE AUDITOR

A solid basis is indispensable for implementing any audits successfully. Auditors constitute significant success factors during this process. The first and most important question refers to the self-concept of the auditor.

The identification of potentials for improvements within the organization is a crucial job of any auditor. The following tasks are part of that:
- Detecting, documenting, and assessing any deviations
- Recognizing possibilities for optimization in terms of a CIP when it comes to internal auditors
- Collecting information which has to be correct, provable, and relevant for the very objective of the audit

There are special requirements on communication during remote audits since the auditor must make sure that
- There is a positive atmosphere during the audit conversation
- Communication is matter-of-fact, objective, businesslike, and characterized by an orientation toward actual tasks
- No personal comments are made on the competency or person of the auditee.
- Interaction is shaped by a sense of partnership
- The auditor is continually motivated to provide the audited party with what needs to be reported.

2.1. THE AUDIT

The term *"audit"* stems from the Latin word *"audire"*, which means, *"to listen, to hear"*. Understanding and processing what has been said and checking back in a targeted and purposeful way are among basic requirements on good auditors.

Following DIN EN ISO 19011, audits are defined as systematic, independent, well-structured, and well-documented processes for evaluating objectively whether the respective audit criteria have been fulfilled and for providing the corresponding evidence if they have actually been met.

The differentiation among the various kinds of audits is particularly relevant here. As stated in DIN EN ISO 19011, there are 3 different types of audits:

First Party Audits

These audits can be performed by internal or externally hired auditors. As a rule, they should be conducted by internal auditors, who can be assisted and supported by external ones.

Second Party Audits

They can be performed by internal or external auditors. Typically, this term refers to supplier audits.

Third Party Audits

These audits are conducted by external auditors, more precisely speaking, by certification auditors. DIN EN ISO/IEC 17021-1:2015-11[14] applies to these audits.

Internal audits refer to the respective organization itself and are performed within the organization. An external auditor very often provides the possibility to obtain an independent and neutral evaluation. This

---

[14] https://www.beuth.de/en/standard/din-en-iso-iec-17021-1/231355332

is not to say that internal auditors would handle things differently, but people do frequently miss the forest for the trees.

Insuring independence may constitute a challenge, especially when it comes to auditing company top management, and external auditors can provide support in doing so.

Basically, audits are valuable tools for improving and further developing quality management. The current state of affairs can be checked by audits, and enhancements may be suggested, based on the experience of the auditor.

In spite of this, audits are very often perceived as tests or examinations. People feel really frequently that auditors just want to question them, sound them out, and use their answers against them.

Put special emphasis on possible improvements!

3rd Party Audits go together with special requirements. Based on ISO 17021, an attestation of conformity is what they are about. That means, the certification auditor checks whether the organization has been abiding by the relevant standards and legal regulations. If so, the organization will obtain a certificate confirming that they have been acting in a manner conform to a certain standard, for instance DIN EN ISO 9001, and that they have been certified accordingly.

It is important that the organization issuing the certificate is accredited, that means, for example, by the DAkkS[15], when it comes to Germany. The organization issuing a certificate needs to be accredited in some other sectors. In the automotive branch, this requirement is governed by the industry-specific IATF 16949:2016-10 standard[16].

---

[15] https://www.dakks.de/en

[16] https://www.beuth.de/en/technical-rule/iatf-16949/263942493

There is another differentiation among audits, as follows. There are

Combined Audits

Provided that several standards have been implemented by one organization, conformity to those various standard requirements may be examined during one single audit. Especially the new high level structure facilitates this type of audit.

In practice, that will make sense, for instance if and when standard requirements in common stemming from an environmental audit (ISO 14001), a quality management audit (ISO 9001), and a data privacy audit (ISO 27001) are supposed to be audited during one single audit.

Audit the same or similar standard requirements during one single audit.

Collaborative Audits

During collaborative audits, one organization is audited by at least two other organizations.

In practice, that may be the case if it is found during a supplier audit that, for example, an important structural component is manufactured by a sub-supplier.

A collaborative audit may be conducted on the sub-supplier's premises in order to check if this sub-supplier is able to provide good quality. To that purpose, the supplier schedules an audit with their supplier and takes their customer along to the audit in order to have the said customer also audit the sub-supplier.

It is important to keep in mind that the audit is always tantamount to a random test and does not constitute a 100 % examination, though.

The success of an audit depends on the experience of the auditor who is doing the job and on their ability to assess what they have seen, based on their experience and the given standards and directives.

Nonetheless, an audit equals a random test, meaning a snapshot in time during which a focus area defined in advance and being the subject matter of the audit is checked for conformity and compliance.

2.2. REMOTE AUDITING PRINCIPLES

Remote audits should have no other bases here than those defined for audits according to DIN EN ISO 19011. These 7 principles are briefly listed subsequently:

Integrity
Integrity is the bedrock of working professionally as an auditor. That means being honest and making ethical decisions. Each and every auditor must be aware of their responsibility as an auditor.

In practice, that means that auditors shall perform solely the auditing activities they are competent to conduct. This requirement has already been adopted as a mandatory condition by other standards, for instance, by VDA 6.3[17]. Pursuant to VDA 6.3, an auditor must prove their auditing competency, or else they may not perform the respective audit.

Factual presentation
Factual presentation means the obligation to present the results precisely, exactly, and without any assumptions.

As Managing Director of PeRoBa[18] Unternehmensberatung (Management Consultancy) GmbH (LLC), the author adopted this principle as a value maxim and guideline for his company, stating, *"We don't waste time and we limit ourselves to the essentials."*

> *<Figures, dates, and facts> instead of*
> *<Mere general discussions>*

Adequate professional care and diligence
This requirement means that auditors must exercise the necessary professional diligence and due care, meaning that regarding their assess-

---

[17] https://webshop.vda.de/QMC/en/e-band-6-teil-03-2016-2
[18] https://www.peroba.de/

ments and during the respective situations, they have to take all the neccessary influences into account and thus, come to well-founded evaluations.

Confidentiality
Auditors will obtain a lot of information on the job. Part of this organizational data is confidential or stems from talking to employees of the organization.

Auditors must protect, uphold, and maintain confidentiality when it comes to utilizing that information. In practice, that means no finger-pointing!

Information that has been obtained during an auditing conversation must be proven by auditors through objective evidence in the aftermath of the audit. Good external auditors point out on their own that a non-disclosure agreement (NDA) needs to be signed.

Independence
Auditors are supposed to come to auditing conclusions in a manner which is independent, impartial, and objective.

Thus, they are required to assess and evaluate in a way that is free of prejudice of any kind.

A fact-based approach to making decisions
Auditors are not supposed to assess or make decisions based on mere presumptions, but on existing evaluations, statistics, and evidence on a rational level.

A risk-based approach
That means that the process is supposed to be carried out in a risk-based manner, as regards planning, actual performance, and completion of the audit.

In practice, this may entail the consequence that high-risk areas within the auditing program have to be audited more often.

As to that, the author has a motto which he likewise tries to impart to participants during the training for auditors at the TÜV Süd Academy:

"The risks that have not been detected are the worst."

2.3. REMOTE AUDITING SKILLS

The skills required of auditors are postulated by different sets of regulations and must be defined on one's own responsibility. As a matter of principle, auditors need methodological, professional / technical, social, and personal abilities.

The author is a member of the German Federal Association of Auditors and of their task force on determining the requirements on the skills required of auditors. Especially when it comes to conducting fully remote audits, there will be higher requirements on the skills of the auditors, compared to on-site audits.

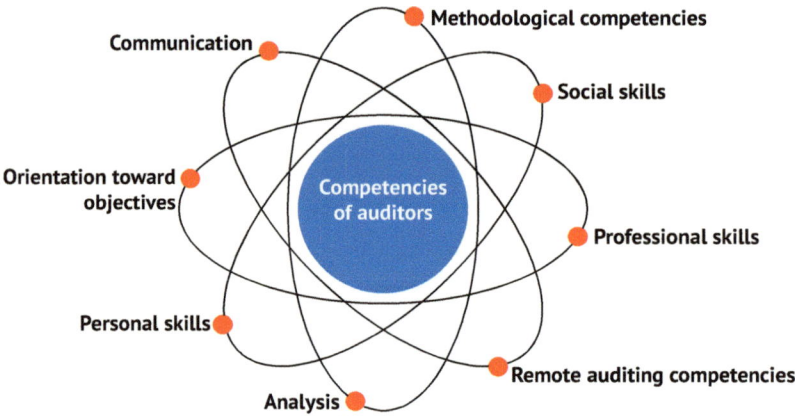

Figure 5: Competency overview

Auditors need to meet the following requirements in terms of **methodological capabilities**:
- Conducting conversations that are oriented toward objectives and results in accordance with the respective auditing assignment
- Applying a professional auditing practice and mastering the regulatory circuit of the auditing process pursuant to ISO 19011
- Documenting and presenting results
- Assessing and prioritizing based on objective evidence

The subsequent **social skills** are required of auditors:
- Acting in an appreciative way toward the audited party and members of the auditing team
- Tolerating and resolving conflicts respectively mediating in case of conflicts
- Giving feedback
- Not being SELF-absorbed but able to work in a team
- Being empathetic and diplomatic
- Integrating cultural differences

Auditors need the following competencies in the **professional respective technical departments**:
- Having good knowledge of the standards pursuant to which they perform their respective audits
- General knowledge of the company structure as well as of workflow management / process organization / methods and procedures
- From their professional experience, they regularly need to know the activities, structure, culture, and management of the organization
- Interpreting legal provisions and contractual terms
- Evaluating the relevance of specific framework conditions and interested parties
- Having sector and technology-specific know-how

The subsequent **analytical competencies** are requirements auditors need to fulfill:
- Researching and presenting information
- Appraising and evaluating facts and circumstances against the backdrop of their own and others' interests
- Differentiating among assertions that either state, explain, or evaluate something
- Assessing principles, mathematical correlations, and statistics

SPECIFIC	MEASURABLE	ACHIEVABLE	REALISTIC	TIME-RELATED
Target a specific area for improvement.	Quantify or at least suggest an indicator of progress.	Specify who will do it.	State what results can realistically be achieved, given available resources.	Specify when the result(s) can be achieved.

Figure 6: The SMART criteria, as described by George T. Doran

The following **personal skills** are necessary for auditors to have:
- Being upright and sincere
- Having a self-confident demeanor and standing to their opinions
- Being open-minded and taking alternative views
- Working reliably and precisely
- Being committed and dedicated as well as possessing stamina and staying power
- Having a sense of humor
- Being quick-witted and attentive
- Acting in a responsible, accountable, and ethical manner
- Having "ankle biter"-abilities in order to pursue issues and topics resolutely

Auditors need the subsequent **goal attainment competencies**:
- Planning for decision-making bases
- Mastering the SMART criteria
- Avoiding pitfalls on the path to goal attainment
- Finding solutions for objectives and aims that have not been achieved yet

The following **communication skills** are to be required of auditors:
- Verbal and non-verbal communication
- Active listening
- Rhetoric

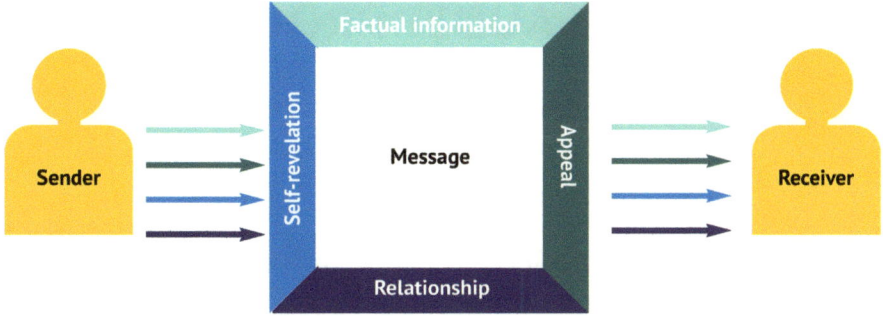

Figure 7: The four-sides model, as described by Friedemann Schulz von Thun

- Language and its impact
- (Knowledge of) stereotypes
- Dealing with objections and killer phrases
- The sender-receiver model
- The four aspects of a message
- Effectively using conversational techniques
- Facilitating debates, discussions, talks, and conversations
- Reasoning in a convincing manner

The subsequent higher competencies can be demanded of auditors when it comes to **remote auditing skills**:
- Communication through digital media
- Increased concentration efforts on the part of the auditor and the audited party
- Time management and breaks
- Generating evidence
- (Knowledge of) (especially legal) framework conditions

The author has already performed plenty of remote audits, and based on his experience, he defined the following maxim for himself: *During remote audits, auditors need to be able to*

"see through their ears".

3 THE REMOTE AUDIT PROCESS

The purpose of the first contact is to create, together with the department to be audited, a basis for the detailed planning of the individual audit.

Arranging for a remote audit is the first operational step on the path to actually conducting it. The auditing program of the respective company is the basis for organizing for internal remote audits.

The COVID-19 pandemic in 2020 changed the requirements on the actual performance of audits. Based on traveling restrictions or company directives, especially external auditors had no more access to company premises in order to conduct audits on-site.

As a matter of principle, the remote auditing process should not deviate from a normal auditing process. That means that there are key points which are to be observed, as regards remote performance. However, that doesn't change basic procedures.

Preparation – 1ˢᵗ stage

The technologies / techniques, the scope, and particularly, the objective of the audit are defined during the preparation stage.

If external auditors are hired, an NDA (Non-Disclosure Agreement) should be signed during this stage.

Please note that in some circumstances, relevant remote auditing documents on paper, which serve as evidence of the audited department, might have to be scanned in advance and shown to the auditor through a sharing function if classic communication tools are used as audit solutions.

The author considers the use of a communication tool to be merely a limited implementation of a remote audit.

Audit plan – 2nd stage

The audit ought to be planned following a risk-based approach. In practice, an audit plan that has been used so far can be supplemented by the subsequent criteria, which are relevant for the remote auditing process:

- An agreement on the utilized technique and / or software solution
- Indicating a contact person and their contact details in case the remote auditing connection won't materialize or will get interrupted
- A fallback solution, especially through a telephone conference provided that problems with the connection continue
- Appraising, scheduling, and if need be, adjusting the auditing time according to the remote auditing process requirements

Experience shows that especially, preparation time goes underestimated, resp., not enough time is scheduled for it.

Document review – 3rd stage

During the document review stage, the documents provided are checked out by analogy with the regular auditing process.

It is relevant reviewing the documents as well as evaluating and checking out the most recent audit reports in order to perform the audit efficiently and as effectively as possible.

Based on the document review, a checklist can, then, be prepared for the remote audit. As in any audit, the document review should take into account the size, the type, and the complexity of the organization as well as the objectives of the audit.

Actual performance – 4th stage

The actual performance or implementation of the remote audit can be divided into two different segments.

Stage 4.1

That's the stage for the classic document review together with the audited party and for the ascertainment of auditing evidence. This stage can currently be carried out through communication tools that are customary and available on the market.

Stage 4.2

During regular audits, this performance stage is about the typical "inspection" of the audit premises and the interviews with the parties involved in the audit processes, according to the requirements from the classic auditing process.

The audit report is created pursuant to DIN EN ISO 19011, based on the information and evidence that have been obtained.

Follow-up – 5th stage

The follow-up stage encompasses the creation of the audit report according to DIN EN ISO 19011, based on the actual performance of the audit. The topics and issues that were found are evaluated in the audit report, and a list of measures is provided to the ordering party.

The audit report must state clearly and in no ambiguous terms whether specific things are about any deviations, remarks, or recommendations.

The report is handed over to the audited department, respectively, the party that had ordered the audit. Optionally, it is possible to have a discussion while completing the audit, and it is a great idea to use digital communication tools during that, too.

The REMOTE AUDITING PROCESS can be graphically depicted, as follows:

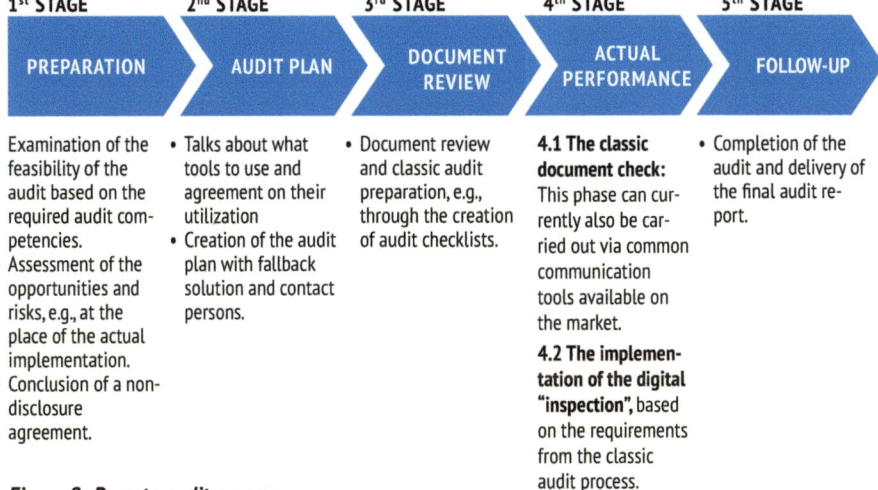

Figure 8: Remote audit process

3.1. THE DEFINITION OF THE REMOTE AUDIT

A remote audit is characterized by the fact that the auditor is not on-site but working at a remote location, which might be, for instance, in an office that is far away. In all other respects, the audit is performed by the auditor just like a classic on-site audit.

The procedures during remote audits are identical to the ones during on-site audits, from the audit planning via the actual performance of the audit and the reporting through to the follow-up. The subsequent examples of remote auditing tools are currently very often listed:

Conference system techniques

They are suitable for conducting interviews and reviewing documents involving the audited department. That step would correspond to stage 4.1 of the aforementioned remote auditing process.

Survey tools and checklists for audit preparation

Partially, they are provided to the audited party beforehand. This way of handling things goes together with both advantages and disadvantages, and to the author, that principle is not indicative of a remote audit yet. Survey tools and checklists are also utilized during on-site audits and supplier audits in order to reduce the auditing time.

Live videos

A live connection is suitable for performing direct interactions with the department that is to be audited. In this context, a livestream can also serve as actual auditing evidence, respectively, it may demonstrate a process result (for instance, a livestream can show and attest to how deficient and faulty products are being scrapped).

Video recordings

Camera and video recordings are suitable as documented information and actual evidence confirming that the audited party is meeting requirements.

3.2. PRECONDITIONS

A stable internet connection with sufficient bandwidth is tantamount to a precondition for performing a remote audit. The bandwidth should be appropriate for a video conference, meaning that transmission through video ought to be viable and feasible without any larger delays or interruptions. This requirement sounds very simple, but nonetheless, it can still constitute a challenge in some parts of Germany right now. Access to speedy internet is very often significantly better abroad than over here when it comes to certain parts of the country or to rural regions.

Furthermore, the necessary technical equipment should be available. The latter can consist of a computer with the respective software for transmitting images and sound (for audiovisual transmission) as well as of mobile devices for receiving and transmitting images and sound (again, for audiovisual transmission).

Both parties, meaning both the auditor and the auditee, need to agree on the procedures. Issues of safety and security as well data privacy and protection are especially relevant and significant when it comes to the utilization of digital technologies.

Insofar as suitable software is used, audit evidence can be documented right away for the report during the actual audit. As to that, it is mandatory making sure that such evidence is managed, administered, and treated pursuant to data protection regulations.

All the other preconditions and requirements are no different from a normal audit. Communication is always key in this case, though.

Contrarily to an audit during which the auditor is personally on-site, they can't take communication through body language into account. During a virtual audit, the latter is regularly not present or only available to a limited degree, as only a partial area, mostly the face, is visible.

So, communication can very often lead to misunderstandings. The auditor must be very well aware of that since they are actually conducting the conversation.

The audited party ought to be aware of this circumstance as well. However, it is the auditor who is actually conducting the conversation – and a conversation without the complete facial expressions and gestures of their counterpart at that!

Other influences might also lead to misunderstandings or a faulty evaluation. Every auditor who performs a remote audit ought to be aware of this circumstance.

Involving specialists is easier. They are solely needed for the point in time when their expertise is called for, and this might lead to significant savings in terms of traveling time and costs.

Make sure that specialists are available.

A crucial precondition for performing remote audits is that the auditor needs to know the organization they are going to audit. From the point of view of the author, completely fully remote audits are not always feasible due to the limitations of the currently available technologies.

This is so, irrespectively of what technique is used. On the contrary, the inspection part also needs to be covered during a fully remote audit, see The Remote Audit Process, stage 4.2.

The utilization of mobile end devices or of data glasses, so-called smart glasses, would constitute a minimum alternative there.

However, these technologies will also be currently stretched to their limits, for instance, whenever other senses like the ones of smell, touch, and taste are needed.

At present, it is not possible to digitally feel sand, which might also be measured by a sand testing machine in a foundry.

For this reason, the author holds a more than skeptical view on remote audits at unknown organizations in terms of the audit performance in accordance with DIN EN ISO 19011.

Assess the risks of the remote audit!

Subsequently, there is a rough outline of the options for use:

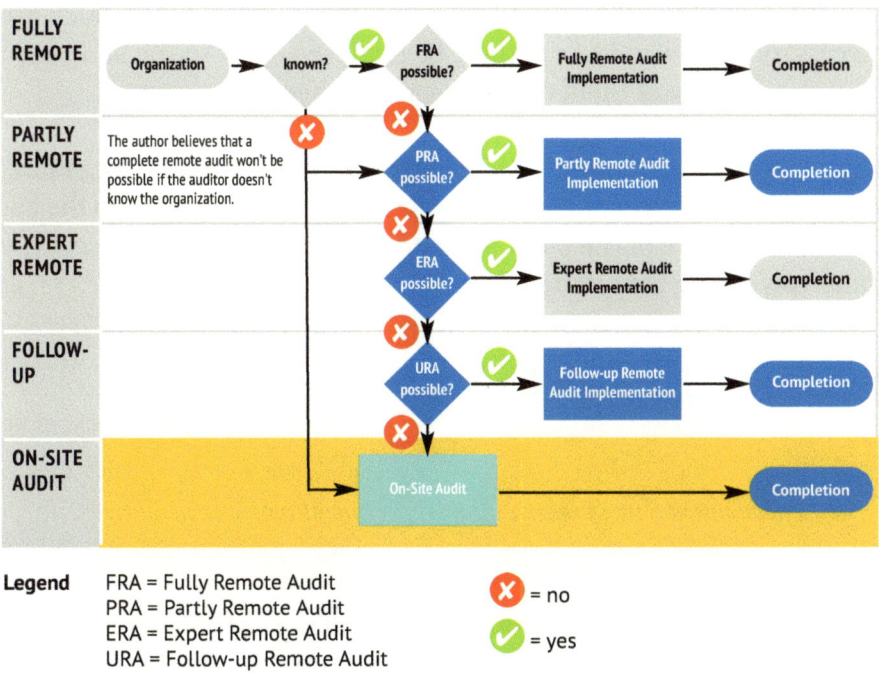

Figure 9: Preconditions

3.3. THE AUDIT PLAN

Furthermore, the audit plan is a relevant document. In a colloquial sense, it is the auditor's agenda, and for the unit that is to be audited, it is an overview of what actions are going to take place in which departments and of how much time is scheduled, among other things.

In the opinion of the author, preparation in terms of a document review is absolutely mandatory before the audit plan can be created.

That means, the first steps to be included in the audit plan are about the definition and objective of the audit along with a clarification regarding the scope of the audit made together with the party ordering the audit.

According to these framework conditions, the documents, process descriptions, and the directives for work and the procedures, which are necessary for the audit, can, then, be made available to the auditor so that they can check them out and evaluate them.

This provides auditors with insight into the processes of the organization, and it might enable them to ascertain risks with regard to the actual performance of the audit so that they can identify and assess the said risks during the audit.

A review of the last audit report, or at least, of the last audit report that is relevant for the audited department should not be forgotten.

> *Check out the most recent audit reports and plans for measures.*

It counts for a principle that the wheel ought not to be reinvented time and again. The findings and experiences of the colleague who performed the previous audit could be helpful for obtaining a first impression.

38

For example, any deviations or measures that the audited department has to carry out should be defined. Then, their compliance can be reviewed during the audit.

In practice, that means that the audited department must remedy any deviations found beforehand through suitable measures, or else, they would then have to come up with a proper justification at this point during the audit at the latest in order to avoid another deviation.

Besides, the names of the auditor, the co-auditors, and the involved parties need to be included in the audit plan. The same is true for a rough outline stating who is going to be audited when, where, and about which issues and topics.

Especially within the context of the remote audit, a passage on the specialties of remote audits should not be absent from the audit plan either. With regard to risk-based audits, this means that planning for possible problems has to be included.

In practice, that may mean that another contact person and their telephone number will be indicated in the audit plan so that the auditor can get in touch with this person if the internet connection or anything else breaks down in any sort or manner.

How can the audit be continued under these framework conditions as a classic audit with a risk-based approach? Is there any person in any role that might assume the responsibility and take over if the auditor can't participate in the audit any more because of any problems? In the automotive branch, this is recommended through the respective directives and guidelines.

The actual performance needs to be taken into special consideration during plans for remote audits. The remote audit might be different here, depending on what solution is used for the remote audit.

If so-called communication tools like, for instance, Teams, Skype, Webex, etc., are used, the respective evidence could be recorded, to be sure, but the audited party must always be told about that clearly and in no ambiguous terms before.

Not all of these methods will enable the audited party to make sure that nothing gets recorded in actual fact, though. That means that in this situation, remote audits require a certain amount of trust in the auditor's and the involved parties' only recording what has been permitted.

This point will be especially relevant if confidential or not generally visible areas or documents are shown at the premises of the audited party.

If specific remote auditing solutions like, for example, iVision® of PeRoBa Unternehmensberatung (Management Consultancy) GmbH (LLC) are used, the requirements on audits over to management systems can be supported through software.

That means that the audited party can automatically detect any recordings made during the audit, irrespectively of whether they are in the form of a screenshot or a video. Utter and utmost transparency can be insured and guaranteed in this manner.

How can confidentiality, safety, and security as well as data privacy and protection be made sure of during remote audits? The legal provisions and regulations and possibly, additional agreements must be abided by here.

Contacting the data protection officer of the organization might be helpful. The directives and guidelines for efficiently implementing safety measures ought to be included in the audit plan.

Audit plan

Client:		
Lead Auditor:	Dr. Roland Scherb / (RS)	Project no .:
Auditor (Expert):	-	Audit date:
Audit officer:		

☐ Trial certification audit	☐ Post-audit	☐ ISO 45001
☐ Surveillance audit	☐ ISO 37301	☐ ISO 29990
☒ Remote Audit	☒ ISO 27001	☐ SCC/SCP
☐ Repeat audit	☒ ISO 9001:2015	☐ ISO 50001
☐ Pre-Audit	☐ ISO 14001	☐ IATF

Audit objectives (Focus)	Carrying out an internal audit - audits are random checks according to the scope and criteria of the audit.	
Remarks:	n.a,	Numb. of employees:
Scope:	☒ see certificate text (see below)	☐ no change

date Time [1]	Processes / area	responsible [2] and standard requirements	Auditors
	Welcome and explanation of the audit plan	ALL	RS
	Discussion and clarification of the system requirements Document and document review level 1 Structure and processes of the QM system		

Created on:		Audit language	

Distribution: customer / auditor / ...
Customer (with the request for internal redistribution)

The audit times are indicative. Depending on the topic and the documents, these can be exceeded or not reached.

Figure 10: Prototype of an audit plan of PeRoBa GmbH (LLC)

3.4. PREPARATION

The preparation for any remote audit is basically identical to the one for any on-site audit. Close attention should be paid to the technology, the techniques, and the surroundings while preparing for any remote audit.

Especially on condition that an audit takes place in a different time zone and is therefore subject to time-shifts, the auditor will have to work outside their regular hours.

Good lighting, respectively, illumination at the workplace is part of basic requirements. Please make sure to heed the regulations under labor law also, as from our practice, it could be observed time and again that for instance, light sources were directly shining into the faces – and thus, into the very eyes of people.

That can lead to stronger fatigue, tiredness, and exhaustion. Indirect background lighting would be optimal, as in this manner, the auditor can be very well recognized on the picture on the one hand, and the working surface is well illuminated for notes, on the other hand.

On top of that, the workplace of the auditor ought to be quiet and tidy, as the auditor is sitting in front of the computer and conducting the audit virtually. Having a quiet workplace should also mean here that any unintended and inadvertent disruptions by other people in the background will be avoided, especially if and when the audit pertains to sensitive areas and data. Meanwhile, there are also mobile backgrounds, which can be flipped open in order to conceal the rear view.

As an auditor, you need to be aware of the audited party focusing and concentrating on you during the audit. The utilization of any unsuitable virtual backgrounds might also prove disruptive during audits.

For performing remote audits, the author uses a PC with two external cameras, an external high-quality microphone, two external loudspeakers, and four monitors that are connected to the PC.

The external microphone and the loudspeakers can likewise be omitted in accordance with other personal preferences if a good headset is utilized instead.

One PC camera is used for talking to the audited party with the aid of the respective software, and the second camera is utilized for presentations on a flip chart in order to point out correlations, etc.

> *The use of "classic" auxiliary means, like, for instance, flip charts, whiteboards, etc., can also be helpful during a digital audit.*

The monitors fulfill different functions during the remote audit:
- Contents are shared with the auditor, talked over, and discussed on **monitor 1**.
- The audited party is shown on **monitor 2** so that both parties can see each other. Please make sure to look into the camera while speaking, as this can convey the impression of having eye contact. Holding the camera in the correct manner is also crucial. Avoid positioning the camera too far below, as this conveys the impression of an image from above to the audited party, and it can, therefore, also prove disruptive to the auditing process.

> *Mark the camera with an eye-catching symbol that reminds you to speak into the camera.*

- Relevant Word or PDF files are shown in portrait mode on **monitor 3**.

- On **monitor 4**, an interaction tool or alternatively, Outlook or a notes application is presented to the participants in the audit.

Again, you must perform the respective tests in advance in order to make sure that you can achieve the effects you want to create during the audit. Especially the technology check, which has been mentioned several times before, is important. As a matter of principle, there can never be too many tests.

Nothing is worse than detecting that a technique or a functionality is not working while you are amidst an audit you are conducting.

Of course, you can always say, "It never works while somebody is watching!", but professional remote audit performance also places special demands on the auditor.

A remote audit is supposed to be conducted in as professional a manner as an on-site audit. That's the aspiration to strive for here.

The author strongly disagrees with some recommendations on the internet claiming that the success of any remote audit is supposedly dependent on creating and using checklists and on sending them over to the audited department for self-assessments in advance.

Of course, it may prove advantageous to send a self-assessment checklist to the audited party, as that can help to save time during the performance of the actual audit. However, it should be taken into account that in this case, the audited party can, then, prepare for the audit accordingly, as forewarned is forearmed.

Therefore, it is possible that certain failings can be detected during the audit if you don't provide the checklist beforehand.

Subsequently, there is an overview of the preparation stage:

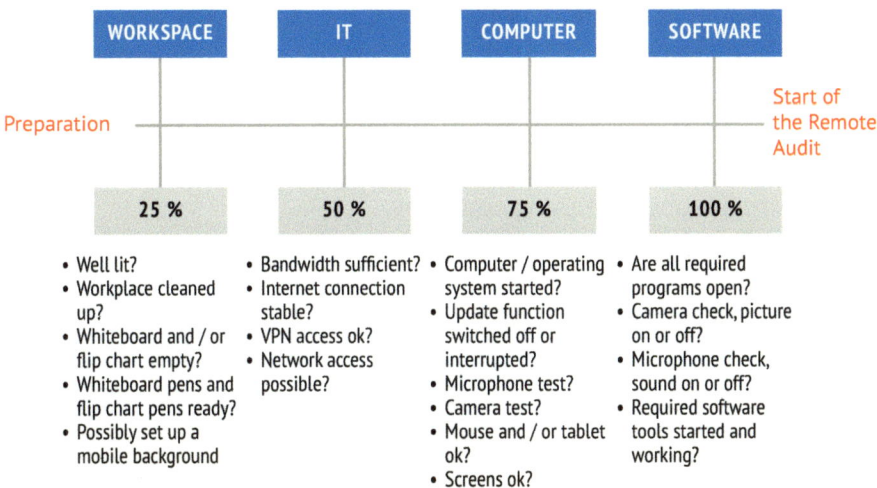

Figure 11: Remote audit preparation

3.5. PERFORMANCE OF THE AUDIT

As a matter of principle, the remote auditing process will remain identical, irrespectively of whether the remote audit is conducted on the premises of a manufacturing company or within the service sector.

The requirements on the remote audit or the complexity are different, though. The production floor and the workshops, etc., also need to be audited at a manufacturing company. In the service sector, the place where the actual services are rendered might need to be audited in an analog manner. For instance, the vehicles may have to be audited when it comes to a mobile cleaning company.

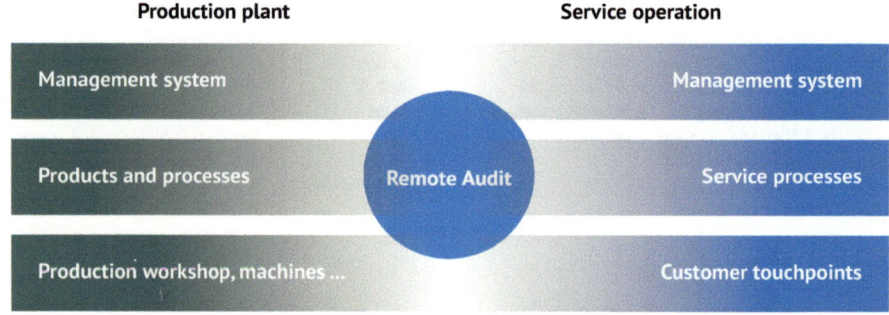

Figure 12: Remote audit performance

According to the remote auditing process, a decision has to be made about during which stage this gets carried out, meaning, whether this is done during the "document review" stage 4.1 or during the "inspection" stage 4.2.

The existing techniques can be used for the document review stage 4.1, as explained before. Regarding inspection stage 4.2, current technologies could be stretched to their limits, though.

The available techniques for video conferences and document sharing, like, for instance, MS-Teams, Webex, Skype, Jitsi, GoToMeeting, Zoom, etc., are suitable for document review stage 4.1.

The respective functionalities for presenting different documents at the same time, in order to discuss them together and have the auditor explain any queries, are required. As the auditor and the audited party are sitting in front of the PC and conducting the audit virtually, the auditor must pay attention to speaking clearly and slowly, and if necessary, to taking different cultures into account.

During inspection stage 4.2, the demands on the auditor are even greater, as the production floor or other areas have to be inspected, and coworkers who are involved in the respective processes must be questioned.

The author is of the opinion that as a matter of principle, a fully remote performance is not possible at an unknown organization, as described in the previous chapter.

During any remote audits, clear and unambiguous communication with any respective counterpart(s) is definitely always necessary. Please observe likewise all the other rules and guidelines for auditing. That means, do ask open questions.

That doesn't mean that the auditor may only ask open questions, though. For from time to time, asking closed questions can also be very expedient and helpful. This could make sense if the audited party is a very eloquent person or "is always beating around the bush", in colloquial terms.

The auditor can interrupt this process and cause a YES / NO decision through a closed question. If the auditor needs a certain piece of evidence for performing an examination, the auditee will have only two options for answering:

- Either the reply is <NO>. Then, the assessment is up to the auditor.

- If the answer is <YES>, the auditor can request documented information as evidence and has interrupted a discussion that had led nowhere through this approach.

The auditor should not forget to thank the audited party for their time when they have completed their questions.

The auditing process is always a disruptive one. Therefore, it is certainly adequate thanking the audited party for their time and cooperation. Furthermore, appreciation can also be helpful for strengthening the acceptance of audits within the company over the long haul.

> *Summarize at the end of the audit and of your questions.*
> *Thank the auditee for their support.*

Summarize briefly both when you are through asking individual questions as well as after the entire audit. The auditor points out clearly how the audit went and what deviations were found.

That needn't always mean that the auditor will approach the audited unit on grounds of deviations and with demands.

It is very expedient and efficient to name positive effects first thing.

The objective of an audit is not always about finding any deviations, but it is mainly about insuring and guaranteeing improvements and conformity to standard requirements.

Positive things should be pointed out primarily and included in the audit report by the auditor.

Subsequently, there is a summary of the actual performance of the audit and of relevant influences:

AUDIT STAGE	OBJECTIVE	REQUIREMENT DURING THE REMOTE AUDIT	
INTRODUCTION	• Welcoming participants and brief explanation of the reason, scope, purpose, etc. • If necessary, establish and explain communication rules	Auditor	• **Lead the conservation!** Speak slowly and clearly.
		Tools	• Explain the rules of communication, for example, all participants have the microphone off, except for the conversation partner.
		Communication	• At the beginning, ask whether the communication is okay. • Finally, give a short summary, and ask whether there are any points that are not clear.
IMPLEMENTA-TION	• Don't ask just the managers but also the employees involved. • Speak clearly and slowly and look into the camera, not the monitor! • Ask whether recordings for verification purposes are allowed and do not take them on your own. • Clearly state any deviations.	Auditor	• Ask more often whether the communication is okay and you are well understood.
		Tools	• Look at the camera! If the bandwidth is insufficient, deactivate the camera (only possible in phase 4.1).
		Communication	• Present a short summary, and have a break after an hour at the latest.
		Strategy	• Stop dividing the screen if there is no document, etc., to be discussed. Show only the **relevant thing.**
COMPLETION	• Summary and thanks • Name positive things and deviations • Refer to the audit report and to how any recorded information is handled.	Auditor	• Thank the auditees, and summarize your impressions.
		Communication	• No finger-pointing and no "it was the technology to blame"…

Figure 13: Audit performance overview

3.6. FOLLOW-UP

The follow-up comes after the completion of the remote audit. Now the decision about the selection of the respective remote auditing software is relevant.

If classic communication software is used, handwritten notes must be taken during the audit and integrated into the audit report afterward.

Recorded information that has been permitted, as the case may be, must now be matched with the corresponding assessment points and also be included in the report. In a supplementary manner, checklists that have been filled out in advance may provide support in creating the final audit report.

The audit report must contain a summary of the audit together with the findings and also an evaluation.

Especially with regard to remote audits, the auditor must insure that any digitally recorded information be treated pursuant to data protection regulations.

That means that any strangers or unauthorized persons must not be able to access any auditing evidence or information. The auditor ought to promptly delete any irrelevant information, respectively, any other documents that were recorded over any other circumstances and that are not relevant for the audit.

The question of how this data ought to be handled arises after the completion of the entire audit.

4 A PRACTICAL EXAMPLE OF A REMOTE AUDIT PERFORMANCE

The author was hired for an on-site audit in China in 2018. The outbound flight took place on Sunday so that the audit could begin on Tuesday.

The audit was scheduled for three days (from Tuesday to Thursday), and the auditing results were supposed to be presented on Friday. The return flight took place on Friday evening, and the arrival in Germany was on the weekend.

It rained heavily during the return trip on Friday, which caused flight cancelations and delays. Therefore, the connecting flight in Beijing could not be reached, and an additional overnight stay became necessary. The next possible flight was not before Saturday night, and the arrival in Germany took place on Sunday evening.

This type of assignment was the reason for the decision to conduct digital aka remote audits with the aid of the respective software. For the first remote audits, an in-house invention from 2014 called iVision®[19], with data glasses from the logistics department, was used.

During that process, data glasses would be worn. Images and sound could be transmitted, and supplementary information could be sent to the person wearing those data glasses through augmented reality (AR).

The first audits, during which different data glasses were used, based on this new and inventive technique, were of interest to auditees, to be sure, but from our experience, they haven't gained general acceptance so far.

The author was aware of the fact that this solution had originally not been developed for utilization during audits. But the functionalities

---

[19] https://www.i-vision.eu/

provided a lot of common aspects and congruities, which supported the actual performance of remote audits.

The subsequent table shows a rough overview of the said feedback:

ADVANTAGES	DISADVANTAGES
• Mobile use possible	• Very good WiFi coverage is required
• Various application possibilities if data glasses support camera, sound, WLAN, scanner, etc.	• Battery life approx. 45 minutes or up to 1.5 hours, depending on the application
• With an additional battery, the runtime can be extended for up to approx. 1 hour	• Low acceptance, as a cable and spare batteries have to be carried along when using the glasses
	• Acceptance of the data glasses was low, especially when used for a long time, due to their weight and comfort issues
	• Wearing problems for people with glasses depend on the data glasses used.

Figure 14: Use of data glasses advantages / disadvantages

On a presentation during the CeMAT in Hanover in 2016, the use of these data glasses with the aid of Vuzix M100 was demonstrated.

The author is wearing Vuzix data glasses on figure number 15.

The display in the background showed the occurrences that had been made to happen through the aforementioned data glasses. Accordingly, the visitors at the fair could pursue on the monitor what the person wearing the data glasses was seeing.

Figure 15: Data glasses application example

The users were led through the process with the aid of AR information, and they could all solve the task at hand successfully.

Subsequently, there is a screenshot of an application example, which demonstrates how the built-in scanner read the barcode of a sample bottle and checked it for correctness with the aid of its connection to the warehouse system:

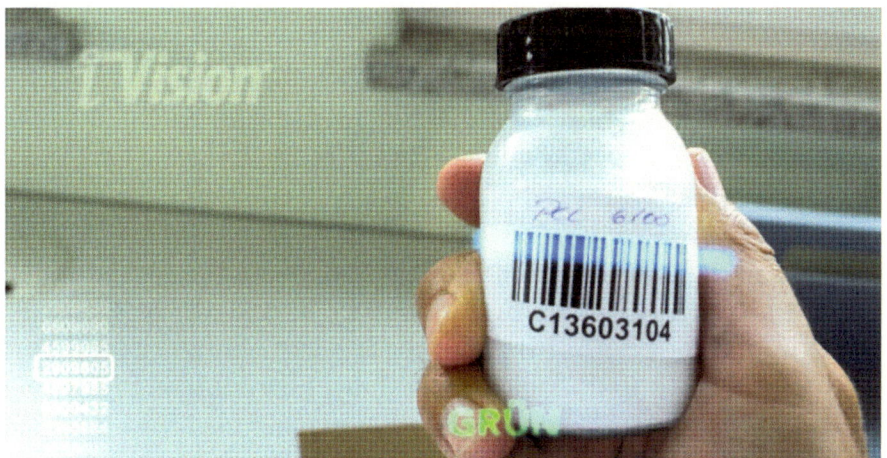

Figure 16: Application example for the use of data glasses

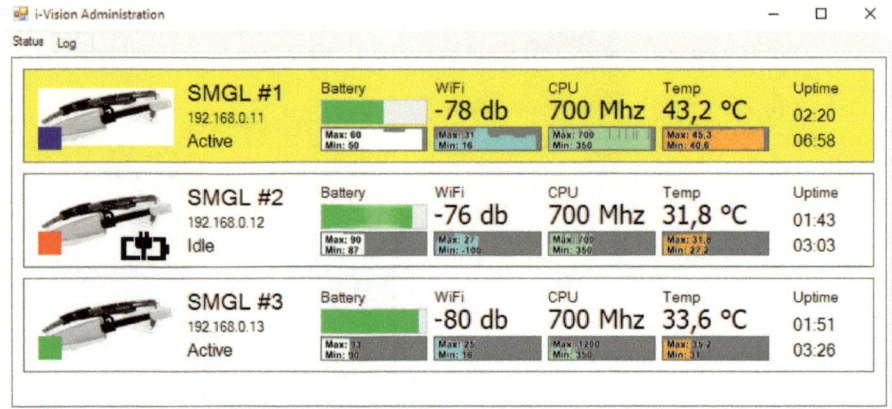

Figure 17: Administration overview

The user was shown the following feedback:

- **GREEN** for OK or
- **RED** for NOT OK

through AR. This was administered, performed, and processed on the PC used for monitoring functions during remote audits.

Since the said data glasses did not meet with that much of a positive response on the part of the users, the author further developed the application explicitly for audits.

To that purpose, it was of primary importance that any mobile terminals could also be utilized.

That means that any mobile end devices may be used, irrespectively of whether they are Android or iOS products. The auditor has a user interface of their own supporting auditing requirements pursuant to DIN EN ISO 19011. The following example shows how our remote auditing solution, iVision®, is used on the cellphone and how the examined item, the CAT5 cabeling on port 7, is transmitted.

54

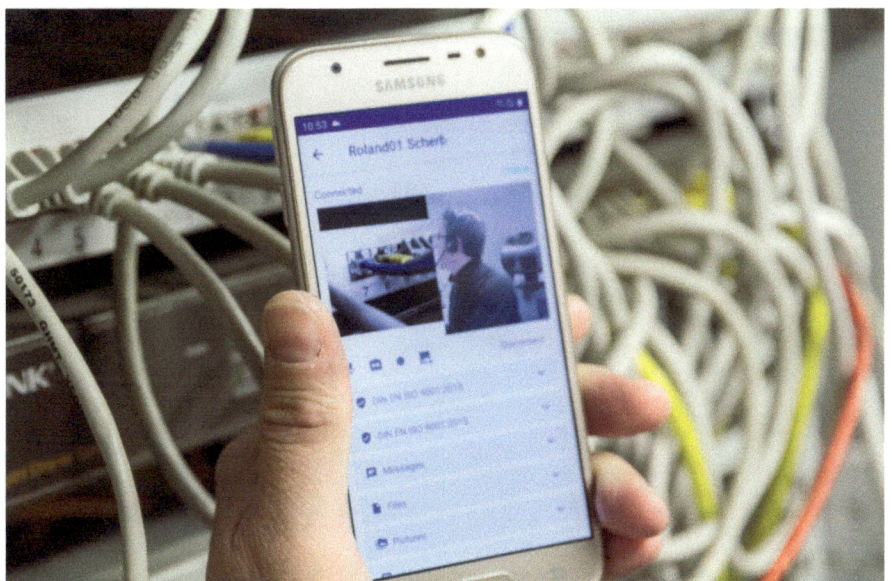

Figure 18: Application example regarding remote audit

The right side of the monitor shows the auditor, who is communicating with the auditee on-site, who is holding the cell phone.

A comparable audit overseas can be performed with the aid of this remote auditing solution – and without any traveling time and costs at that!

The subsequent page presents an overview of an overseas audit, clarifying the cost advantages that go together with conducting remote audits in places beyond the sea.

INTERNATIONAL AUDIT	ON-SITE AUDIT		iVISION REMOTE AUDIT	SAVINGS
		Efforts	Efforts	
PREPARATION	Office	1 day	0.5 day	
IMPLEMENTATION	On-Site	2 days	2 days	
	Travel time	2.5 days	–	
	Travel expenses[20]	8.560 €[21]	–	
POST-PROCESSING	Office	1 day	1	
TOTAL AMOUNT OF TIME	Time	6.5 days	3.5 days	3 days
TOTAL COSTS	Costs	8,560 €	760 €	7.800 €

Figure 19: Remote / on-site audit costs comparison

The other accompanying effects constitute even more advantages due to the use of remote audits. No flight had been necessary, which was good for environmental protection. Besides, the time coworkers spent traveling had been reduced, and that provided the company with the opportunity of having them available to work on different assignments, among other things.

The COVID-19 pandemic further reinforced this development in 2020, as meanwhile working remotely – irrespectively of whether from home or from any other place – has almost become standard.

---

[20] Travel costs: transfer costs, flight costs, hotel costs, etc.

[21] Actual costs for an employee on-site from a customer project

5 SUMMARY

In the future, the world of audits can't be imagined without remote audits any more, as they provide an efficient and resource-friendly auditing method.

The associated advantages will prevail over the present limitations on condition that remote audits are prepared for and performed by persons who have the respective skills and capabilities.

Due to developments in other areas, auditing, especially remote auditing, might also gain more importance yet. As of now, e.g., two legislative changes are being planned in Germany for 2021:
- The law on supply chains, and
- The law for strengthening integrity within the economy.

The requirement of testing whether suppliers conform to directives and guidelines can be facilitated by the use of remote audits, especially those which have not been announced beforehand. This is an efficient and promising approach for checking if an external partner does actually meet requirements.

That can also be implemented by small enterprises and even by the smallest companies even though larger businesses are often said to have an advantage over them because of their structures. Environmental concerns will also further advance this issue, as the author could gain the insight over globalization that in part, companies with manufacturing plants abroad must have so many employees commute back and forth that it might take entire airplanes to do so.

Auditors who perform remote audits will need the necessary technological knowledge and the ability to conduct remote audits on top of their professional, methodological, and social skills.

Suitable technological help can decrease the requirements on remote audits.

LIST OF FIGURES